The STORY of CHRISTMAS

illustrated by
NORMA GARRIS

The Standard Publishing Company, Cincinnati, Ohio. A division of Standex International Corporation
© 1996 by The Standard Publishing Company. Printed in the United States of America
ISBN 0-7847-0513-5. All rights reserved. Designed by Coleen Davis

Scripture taken from the International Children's Bible, New Century Version.
© 1986, 1989 by Word Publishing, Dallas, Texas 75039. Used by permission.

Mary was engaged to marry a man named Joseph.
Luke 1:26, 27

An angel told Mary, "You will give birth to a son, and you will name him Jesus. He will be the Son of God."
Luke 1:30-32

Mary and Joseph traveled to Bethlehem to be counted.
Luke 2:4

When they arrived, there were no rooms left in the inn.
Luke 2:7

Mary and Joseph had to stay in a stable with the animals.

**That night, Mary's baby was born. She wrapped
the baby with cloths and laid him in a feeding box.**
Luke 2:6, 7

That night, some shepherds were in the fields
taking care of their sheep. An angel of the Lord
appeared to them.

The angel said, "Today your Savior was born
in Bethlehem! He is Christ the Lord. You will find
him wrapped in cloths and lying in a feeding box."

Then the sky filled with angels who began praising God.
Luke 2:8-13

The shepherds hurried into Bethlehem.
They found Mary and Joseph and baby Jesus.

Everything was just as the angel had said.
Luke 2:16, 17

Wise men came from far away, looking for Jesus.
They had followed his star all the way to Bethlehem.
Matthew 2:1, 2

When the wise men found Jesus, they worshiped him and gave him gifts of gold, frankincense, and myrrh.
Matthew 2:11

"For God loved the world so much that he gave his only Son. God gave his Son so that whoever believes in him may not be lost, but have eternal life."

John 3:16